A Place to Talk

FOR TWO YEAR OLDS

Elizabeth Jarman

Published 2013 by Featherstone, an imprint of Bloomsbury Publishing plc
50 Bedford Square, London, WC1B 3DP
www.bloomsbury.com

ISBN 978-1-4081-9244-3

A CIP record for this publication is available from the British Library.

Printed and bound in China by C&C Offset Printing Co Ltd, Shenzhen,
Guangdong

10 9 8 7 6 5 4 3 2 1

Contents

Introduction 4
Five environmental factors to consider 5
Twelve ideas to try 7

A transformed concrete space 8
A relaxing space 12
Appropriate physical challenge in outside spaces 14
Messy mixing 16
A recycled space 18
Boards and mirrors 20
Pallet space 22
Planting 25
Betsy and Dougie 28
Transition into a setting 30
Mud kitchen 32
Family seating 34

Action points 36
Useful resources 38
Further references and websites 39
About the author 40

Introduction

Two year olds, just as other children and indeed adults, respond strongly and often immediately to the environment in which they find themselves. We shouldn't therefore be surprised at the negative response from often lively two year olds, who are fast developing language, independence and mobility when they find themselves in an environment which doesn't support their interest in exploring and experimenting.

The experiences that children have as they grow and develop are extremely significant in determining the kind of people they will become, so it is crucial to get the physical and emotional environment right. Adults who are open to the messages two year olds are sending and who have a sound understanding of the extraordinary growth and development that takes place during this particular time will be able to create the kind of environment that best supports each child's individual needs today, tomorrow and beyond.

A Place to Talk for Two Year Olds considers the major role that the physical environment can play in supporting two year olds' speaking and listening skills, their emotional well-being and their desire to investigate, stretch boundaries and to understand the world. The book also explores how the environment can be organised to promote positive responses and avoid causing children (and adults!) undue frustration and distress.

This book includes:

- a summary of some of the key environmental influences, collated from research studies
- lots of examples of ways that practitioners and parents/carers have created learning spaces specifically for two year olds which link closely with their developmental needs and their interests
- questions to prompt action
- sign-posts to further information.

The revised *Early Years Foundation Stage 2012* (EYFS) and non-statutory guidance sources such as *Development Matters* and *A Know How Guide* (The EYFS Progress Check at age two)[1] are invaluable legislative and supportive documents to refresh and underpin our knowledge about development, teaching, learning and the central role of adults in children's lives. The good practice identified within them aligns with the real examples in this book which illustrate excellence in action, making a significant positive impact to children and families.

[1] www.education.gov.uk

Five environmental factors to consider

Following a review of research and practice in a wide range of Early Years settings we have identified five particularly important environmental points to consider when creating spaces designed to encourage two year olds' speaking and listening skills. These points are equally important at all stages of a child's education.

1 The physical environment should reflect the pedagogy[1] of the setting.

Establishing a clear understanding of your pedagogy will inform the way that you plan your learning environment. The way that a physical space is arranged communicates a great deal to two year olds about how they are thought about and what is possible there. It's very important that the learning environment and pedagogy connect and support one another.

2 Practitioners should make the most of the space available, both inside and out.

It's important to view learning spaces as a whole, including both inside and out and make the most of what's available. Two year olds need a variety of spaces including comfortable spaces to withdraw to and spaces that facilitate solitary or parallel play. Contained spaces are very significant for this age group and outdoor spaces offer boundless possibilities for inquisitive, physically maturing two year olds.

3 Spaces should take account of physical factors (e.g. noise, colour and light) that can impact on how two year olds feel and respond.

Noise

Being in a noisy environment all of the time makes it hard for two year olds to listen and to concentrate. This can have a negative effect on speaking and listening skills, particularly in relation to hearing and therefore learning the difference between speech sounds and exploring new vocabulary or conversation patterns. Excessive noise can also be stressful and cause negative responses from young children.

Colour

Colours need to be chosen carefully as they can affect how two year olds feel and behave. Overly colourful environments can be over-stimulating which in turn can affect behaviour. A more neutral environment will help two year olds to have periods of calm, to listen and to interact.

[1] Pedagogy is your 'teaching' style.

Light

Current research confirms that we are all energised by natural sunlight and that children learn faster in spaces with natural light. Many two year olds enjoy the outdoor environment which can also support their developing physical skills. The curiosity of two year olds means lighting can be used as a magical resource with this age group.

4 The environment should not be over stimulating but should provoke interest and exploration.

Too much choice can be overwhelming for very young children and too many resources, which two year olds love to transport, can create a cluttered environment with no clear focus. Storage options should therefore be carefully considered and the quantity and type of resources should be offered on a developmentally appropriate scale. Curious two year olds find every day and natural objects fascinating and they provide inspiration for thinking and talking.

5 Spaces should be viewed from the child's perspective.

Informed by a thorough understanding of how language develops and each child's unique context, we should keenly observe what two year olds are actually doing and how they are responding to the spaces we create. This helps us to plan appropriate, flexible environments that stimulate speaking and listening skills, encourage appropriate amounts of concentration and engagement, foster relationships with adults and other children of all ages and which reflect their preferred contexts for learning.

We need to step into a child's shoes and imagine how our learning spaces look, feel, sound and smell to them. This enables us to understand their perspective and should inform our pedagogical approach when arranging learning environments.

Twelve ideas to try

Inspired by informed practice from many settings, we have captured twelve 'places to talk' that reflect the five environmental factors.

Each idea is spread over a few pages:

- There is a 'starter' photograph of the space and a description of how it was created.
- We have included some key points about why practitioners selected the materials and resources used.
- There are photographs of children and practitioners using the space, with their comments and some observations of what happened there.
- We have included some action points for you to consider.

You'll see that what we are suggesting doesn't have to cost a fortune. In fact, you may already have some of the materials and resources that we have used. What it does involve though, is an informed view and keen observation skills which impact on planning, so that you create the sort of environment that reflects what you want to facilitate for the two year olds in your setting.

Whilst acknowledging that opportunities for speaking and listening are everywhere, we hope that these ideas will inspire you to review and develop some special 'places for two year olds to talk' in your environment.

A transformed concrete space

HOW AND WHY?

By reviewing all available outside areas you might identify small spaces that are ideal for refurbishment. Large undefined spaces (inside and out) don't always feel 'safe' for two year olds.

This children's centre re-considered their outside space and created some smaller, more manageable areas for their younger children to freely access and explore. A 'dead space' was identified. It was rarely used, had been somewhat overlooked and was in need of refreshing. This small area connected two other outside spaces.

Working with a very limited budget, the team transformed this concrete space into an interesting and inviting area using a range of different natural resources and some recycled materials that appealed to the younger children's current fascinations and interests. These were presented on a scale that the children could manage and enjoy. By working with businesses in their local community to access donations of tyres and logs etc. in total the setting spent just £174. Bark and plants were added to soften the space physically and visually.

Logs are used to create seating and low level display areas. The tyres offer places to investigate and an appropriate physical challenge. The mix of resources made available interested the children, some offering opportunities for transient art.

The area offers a place to concentrate, away from the movement flow, and opportunities to investigate either individually or with a group of friends and supportive interested adults.

Observations of children using this space have clearly shown that for many of the children, outside was their preferred learning context where levels of engagement and focus increased.

Families were keen to understand how their children were learning in this new area and so weatherproofed photos and brief quotes are displayed to explain the learning experiences on offer.

ACTION

Consider the size and scale of the outside spaces for your two year olds and identify areas that might offer a place for them to focus and investigate.

Remember that this could be a permanent or temporary space.

A relaxing space

HOW AND WHY?

Young brains need relaxation as well as activity and stimulus, to help them to develop healthily. Providing spaces for children to refresh, re-group and observe from are essential. As young children absorb what's going on around them they are stocking up using their 'terms of reference', their knowledge of the world. These experiences form an awareness of how the world works and how to operate within it. As we all know, observation is a critical learning mechanism for babies and young children. Additionally, there are occasions when you are very young (and sometimes when you are older!) when it all gets just too much and you need to retreat to somewhere soft and quiet to regulate your emotions.

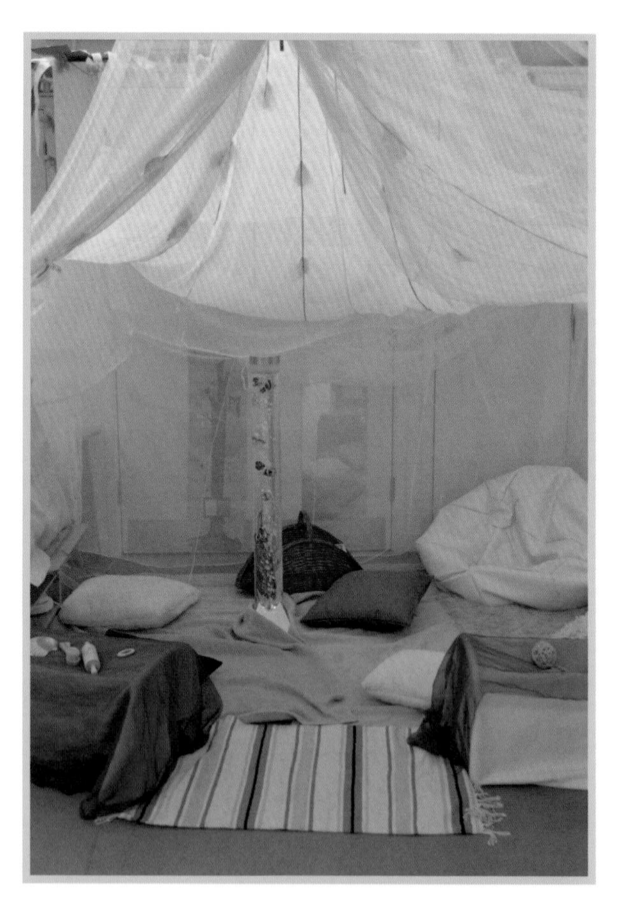

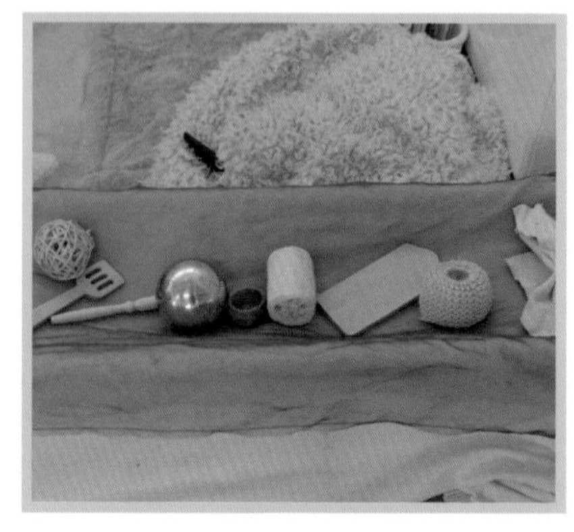

This space has been created with soft materials and screening to define an inviting semi-private area. The drapes lower the high ceiling making it feel quite intimate and child-sized. Interesting resources are available to investigate which connect with several strong observed schemas. There is a manageable selection of familiar books, a warm responsive adult to interact with and a magical light to set the mood. A 'scent maker' contributes a wonderfully calming lemon aroma, suggested by the children who had been investigating lemon balm the week before.

The addition of lighting adds atmosphere. Not only does it illuminate the space but it can also be controlled by the children independently, allowing them to make choices about the 'conditions' they wanted to create.

'Softness' is hugely important in children's environments and so often overlooked. It's also important that comfortable seating for adults is provided for if we want adults to remain engaged with children for periods of time. It was noted that many of the younger two year olds gravitated to this space at the start of each session, using it as a familiar transition point when arriving and separating from their families/carers. They often spent time watching from here until they were ready to join the larger group.

ACTION

Notice where your adults are most engaged with children and how the space enables this to be sustained.

Do your two year olds need a space to 'watch from'?

Appropriate physical challenge in outside spaces

HOW AND WHY?

As two year olds strengthen their muscle groups, increase their heart rates and develop their gross and fine motor skills, physical movement outside often becomes an exciting preferred activity for many. Countless recommendations in the EYFS and associated guidance documents and The British Heart Foundation[1] state that 180 minutes of physical exercise is required daily for children under three once they can walk. Getting the balance right between offering appropriate physical challenge and the time spent enjoying physical play is key.

This outside space has been developed over time, based on observations of the children's preferred play spaces and with the intention to combine physical activity with speaking and listening, investigation, problem solving and learning about cooperative play, supported by engaged adults.

[1] Chief Medical Officers (2011) Start Active, Stay Active: A report on physical activity for health from the four home countries. Department of Health

As the children clambered into the swing they were encouraged to think about how high they were going, how much 'push' was needed to get them there and how far they could stretch out and reach. When they found that they could reach some leaves whilst swinging high they wanted to see if they could also reach the leaves if they were on the ground.

The way that they accessed the swing offered some essential 'tummy time' physical activity, which is critical for brain co-ordination and something lacking in many babies' and young children's early experiences.

The use of materials to make small enclosed spaces in this garden has also been successful and very much enjoyed by the children – some preferring to stay outside of the netting, whilst others bravely venture in, supported by responsive adults.

ACTION

How challenging is your outside space for two year olds?

How can you help them explore their physical limits and capabilities and contribute to their daily requirement for physical activity?

How rich is their speaking and listening outside?

Messy mixing

HOW AND WHY?

Anything 'messy and tactile' is a particular favourite for young children. This pre-school created a novel way to extend this interest through their messy mixing activity.

Recognising the language skills triggered by touching, stirring, spooning, sharing, pouring and 'concocting', staff asked families to sort through their cupboards for any suitable out of date foods. Families also donated old bowls, sieves, crockery, paper cases, baking tins and cooking utensils.

This learning space was set up on a tuff spot on a table so that the children could gather around it in small groups. The positioning facilitated good eye contact with each other as the children talked about their ingredients and recipes. The practitioners did not add chairs to this space as standing around the tuff spot and using upper core muscles of the body is a preferable physical stance for this type of activity.

Supported by knowledgeable adults who described the ingredients to extend vocabulary, the children explored the resources and made their own creations, combining the ingredients. The emphasis was on giving children time to participate and enjoy the process. The concentration on the children's faces, high levels of interest and engagement are evident.

ACTION

How can you involve and interest families in supporting their children's learning?

It's really important to enable children to have plenty of time to become involved in activities and re-visit them when they are ready.

A recycled space

HOW AND WHY?

This is a great example of a simple, free resource that, when blended with a bit of thought, provided a wonderful place to talk and discover. These two sheets of perspex were attached together and then placed in a garden area to form an arch. That in itself created an interesting space for the two year olds as they went through it, pressed their faces against the plastic to see what they could see and traced the grooves with their fingers.

The addition of water added a fascinating element that could be independently managed by the children. Encouraging independence is an important skill that we can weave into the care of two year olds, with supportive scaffolding. Understanding and allowing children to repeat and revisit over and over, to problem solve and test out different solutions, to build resilience and coping strategies when things don't quite go as planned and also to enjoy success are all critical skills for life, not just when you are two.

When adults share the experience with the children this sends a clear message that this activity is worthwhile. The contributions that the adults made and their continued active presence increased the enjoyment and learning for the children. New vocabulary and extended thinking were all introduced in ways that were accessible for the children yet didn't override their ideas.

ACTION

Set yourself a challenge to make a new 'place to talk' with zero cost.

What would really connect with your children and encourage their speaking and listening?

Boards and mirrors

HOW AND WHY?

Resourcing a learning environment for two year olds with mark making opportunities needs careful thought. It's not simply about the actual resources, but also about their location, height, accessibility and how they can be used. Most two year olds are confident mark makers with a range of resources, some intended for mark making and some not! Nevertheless they do have an innate response to share their ideas in a representative way.

One setting expanded their provision for two year olds and thought very carefully about the learning spaces that were going to be accessed by these children. They knew from previous observations that mark making on the move was a successful activity and that using different body positions to get comfortable, to be able to talk and draw was important.

This space was informed by observations, combined with clear understanding of development. It features a wall of low level chalk boards, some large for group use and some individual, with mirrors above each one so that the children can see themselves communicating, see other people and see themselves in action. The walls around the chalk boards and the mirrors were left intentionally free from further visual clutter (posters and displays for example) so that children could focus clearly.

Promoting positive self-image is critical for all children and this example shows just how simply, yet effectively, it can be done.

In a home context, here is another way to represent children's ideas by placing a whiteboard on the floor. Jacky, a childminder, developed this idea as a way of creating group artwork that still allowed individual contributions whilst participating in a mixed age group. The children all gathered round, including Jacky and she drew some central lines down the middle of the whiteboard. The children got started in their artwork space, chatting as a group, concentrating, admiring each other's work and creating together.

ACTION

How can you enable two year olds to experiment and represent their ideas through drawing and mark making in ways that are developmentally appropriate?

How can adults use these situations as opportunities to talk without becoming directive?

Pallet space

HOW AND WHY?

Think of a two year old you know well and you might possibly conjure up the image of a small person who is driven by curiosity, is already demonstrating some schematic preferences in their play and who delights in the co-construction of their play ideas.

This space has been created from a mixture of reclaimed materials and some inexpensive additional items. The main frame has been made out of a wooden pallet and creates a space which is proportionate in size to very young children. This is an important consideration when planning learning environments as the size of a space can help children to feel more emotionally secure. This space has been positioned in the corner of a garden at a slight angle so when the children are in or around it, they are not too distracted by the level of activity in the main garden. Potentially being a difficult space for adults to get into, makes this a particularly appealing place for some children!

The natural colouring of the materials helps the space to blend into the garden. The space isn't static or fixed, it's flexible and can be moved around the garden or taken indoors. The seating suggests that more than one child can access the space, but it can of course be used in many different ways.

Using the slats of the pallets, the practitioners added bamboo drainpipes which were perfect for testing out the observed trajectory schemas that the two year olds were demonstrating in other areas of their play.

They had great fun rolling things down the gutters e.g. balls, sand and water. This developed collaborative skills, turn taking, observation and lots of talk.

ACTION

Make sure that you give two year olds time to understand new concepts and to practise those that they are currently finding most interesting.

Repetitive opportunities really enhance learning and give children the chance to rehearse and perfect their skills.

Planting

HOW AND WHY?

This nursery school and children's centre is based in Inner London surrounded by high rise flats. Few local families have gardens. Supported by local businesses, the nursery re-developed a dead space into an area full of raised beds. Families are able to 'borrow' their own raised bed and grow vegetables and herbs etc. The allotment area can also be accessed at the weekends. This has helped to create a strong sense of community and friendship amongst families.

Childminders regularly use the drop-in sessions at the centre and are encouraged to use the outside facilities to support their children's learning experiences. Learning about growing food is a regular activity and this childminder brought her children to the centre to do some planting in their raised bed. She knows that they enjoy this type of physically creative activity and its one where their language is free flowing and sustained.

They purchased the seedlings on the way to the centre, talked about what they were going to plant, exploring the names of the vegetables and looking at the pictures on the packets. The group talked about the roots and how deep they needed to be under the soil, watered the plants and talked about how tall they might grow.

The physical skills involved in the planting process provided an opportunity for the children in the group to refine their spade control as they needed to gently push down the newly planted items into the soil, providing a wonderful context for new vocabulary. The size of the raised beds meant that there was plenty of room for everyone to get their hands straight in and dirty whilst still being small and contained enough to work collaboratively as a small group.

The final task was to label the plants so that the children could identify them as they grew. The childminder modelled how to write the name of the plant on the plant stick and then the children completed their own and stuck it into the soil.

ACTION

Helping children to understand healthy eating by introducing real experiences means that their awareness moves from something abstract to a more concrete first hand awareness.

Language developed in this way supports deeper comprehension.

Do you have any live resources that grow?

Betsy and Dougie

HOW AND WHY?

Having contact with living creatures can add a different dimension to children's experiences. Many children do not live in homes with pets or have regular access to them through trips for example. Having animals in settings can offer a chance to take responsibility, to understand the patterns of life and to interact with something that moves and needs looking after. It's an opportunity to replicate the nurturing responses that children receive from others.

Children and their families often lead busy lives. It's important that thought is given to creating spaces that, by their very nature, encourage children to be still and deeply engaged, even just for short periods of time.

These two year old boys, Findlay and Thomas, are fascinated by Betsy and Dougie and like to care for them on a regular basis. This is a well-established routine and one that is familiar to the boys. Findlay sat with Betsy on his lap and held her as carefully as he could. He was keen to participate and sat completely still, holding her confidently, stroking her, pointing out things that he found interesting about her and communicating all the time, using a gentle voice. Thomas looked on the whole time, absorbing everything and then got ready to hold Dougie. He chose to sit on the floor where he felt more comfortable.

Whilst an adult was present, their role was one of guiding rather than deciding, effectively giving more responsibility to the children. Some lovely language, reflection and thinking went on. The photos really capture the sense of calm triggered by the animals.

ACTION

Are there specific resources (e.g. living creatures) which your two year olds associate with calmer behaviours?

Is the quantity of their speaking and listening enhanced when they are interacting with these resources? Why?

Transition into a setting

HOW AND WHY?

For many two year olds being separated from their parents/carers can be a traumatic experience. The sense of being 'new' in a place, of not knowing what happens around here, of wondering 'where my things are' and 'when I'm going to be collected' can all affect children's' emotional well-being, settling, engagement and relationships. Likewise for families, separating from their children can be a difficult time as they learn to share their care with Early Years practitioners and trust someone else to work with their children.

The way that separation takes place can affect both the parent/carer and the child for not only the rest of the day, but in the longer term too. We need to think about how we can enable this aspect of the session/day to take place in ways that are emotionally supportive and reassuring.

Jacky, a childminder who works predominantly with two year olds, is very sensitive to the emotional needs of her families. She has carefully observed and considered the transition into her setting for her children and families and has introduced some ways of minimising separation anxiety.

The walk from the road up to the front door is decorated with welly boot flower pots which have been planted by the children and Jacky. This connection to a shared experience makes a good talking point for parents/carers and children.

Even with her front door closed there is a daily welcome message chalked on the doorstep, telling the families that their presence is anticipated and looked forward to. The children have begun to guess what it might say that day or the following one.

On arrival, Jacky, the parents and children sing a special song which is about saying goodbye to their parents/carers. Jacky is aware that this song indicates to the children that they are making the transition into her care and that for the parents/carers it is time for them to leave, safe and secure in the knowledge that their two year olds are settled. This intervention works for everyone and makes this potentially emotional situation increasingly smooth.

A similar song is sung at the end of the session to say goodbye to the children as they leave with their parents/carers. The children understand that this indicates that it's time to go home.

The familiarity of these routines, helps to provide emotional stability and a growing emotional independence for these two year olds and also support for parents too. At the children's developmental stage, where emotional responses are often near the surface, support and practical strategies are needed to help children to make sense of how they feel.

ACTION

Do you know the points in the children's and family's day which are most stressful and potentially difficult to manage?

What could you do to offer supportive ways to help them all develop strategies to manage this?

Mud kitchen

HOW AND WHY?

This setting made their own mud kitchen with twigs and sticks (collected from the local woods), rope, some camouflage netting, donated saucepans, bowls, sieves and containers and of course mud!

The two year olds in this setting preferred being outside. Staff had noticed that the children's curiosity and creativity were greater there. Having regularly observed children digging in the soil and playing with the natural resources found in the garden, staff decided to create a mud kitchen to further develop this play.

The adult-sized containers and saucepans were added to the twig shelf structure. They could be filled, stirred, carried, poured and emptied, all ideal physical development activities, encouraging hand-eye coordination and motor control, alongside communication. The weight of the containers with mud or water were really heavy, and required careful and practised handling. The space included an old sink on the floor, which was carefully placed to ensure inclusive access.

A stick has a million uses! Here it was used to stir, slice, point, cut, balance, transport and mix. When the stick didn't work, the fingers did! A full body experience and one that these two year olds were deeply engaged in for long periods of time.

ACTION

Do your two year olds have access to opportunities where they can replicate adult activities which they have observed?

Being able to represent your ideas, particularly in visual and practical ways, when you don't have lots of language to articulate those ideas is an important consideration.

Family seating

HOW AND WHY?

Making families feel welcome and at ease is something that we can do regardless of the type of setting that we work in or the amount of space that we have. Children notice and sense how the adults around them are feeling and reacting, observing the complexity of relationships and connections which create foundations for successful family engagement. The physical environment plays a major role in sending messages to visitors about how welcome they are and what types of interactions are possible. Helping parents/carers feel physically comfortable is one simple way of signaling to regular users and visitors that you are interested in them spending time with you and that they are welcome. Of course parents/ carers will have their own levels of confidence about joining in, meeting other families, sharing information and so on, but we should think about how our environment is set up to help them to make friends with other parents/carers even when their children aren't present and how our environment might encourage them to linger and stay. It is also particularly important that our learning environment makes an explicit visual welcome and is not simply text based.

In these examples both inside and outside, notice the care that has been taken to present comfortable, soft, clean spaces that make connections with home. Additionally, the spaces around the seating are not overly cluttered, creating a calm atmosphere – somewhere the adults can simply sit, under no obligation to process another piece of information, complete a form or read a poster.

The positioning of furniture has been considered to offer some levels of privacy when discussions/information exchange is taking place and also good natural daylight. This space has been set up to make conversation easier. The seating is almost face to face, supporting eye contact, smiles and to encourage talk.

Child-sized seating enables children to feel welcome and nurtured.

Notice how these areas are neat, tidy and well presented. This represents a pedagogical approach about responsive and respectful partnerships with families.

ACTION

Walk around your setting as if you were a visitor or new family.

What do you see that makes you know that you and your children are welcome here?

Is information presented in ways that make it easy for you to understand and contribute to?

Action points

Here is a summary of some the questions we posed to prompt action. Use them to reflect on the environment that you currently provide for children and to help you focus on making positive changes.

- **Consider the size and scale of the outside spaces for your two year olds and identify areas that might offer a place for them to focus and investigate. Remember that this could be a permanent or temporary space.**

- **Notice where your adults are most engaged with children and how the space enables this to be sustained. Do your two year olds need a space to 'watch from'?**

- **How challenging is your outside space for two year olds? How can you help them explore their physical limits and capabilities and contribute to their daily requirement for physical activity? How rich is their speaking and listening outside?**

- **How can you involve and interest families in supporting their children's learning? It's really important to enable children to have plenty of time to become involved in activities and to re-visit these when they are ready.**

- **Set yourself a challenge to make a new place to talk with zero cost. What would really connect with your children and encourage their speaking and listening?**

- **How can you enable two year olds to experiment and represent their ideas through drawing and mark making in ways that are developmentally appropriate? How can adults use these situations as opportunities to talk without becoming directive?**

- Make sure that you give two year olds time to understand new concepts and to practise those that they are currently finding most interesting. Repetitive opportunities really enhance learning and give children the chance to rehearse and perfect their skills.

- Are there specific resources which your two year olds associate with calmer behaviours? Is the quantity of their speaking and listening enhanced when they are interacting with these resources? Why?

- Helping children to understand healthy eating by introducing real experiences means that their awareness moves from something abstract to a more concrete first hand awareness. Language developed in this way supports deeper comprehension. Do you have any live growing resources?

- Do you know the points in the children's and family's day which are most stressful and potentially difficult to manage? What could you do to offer supportive ways to help them all develop strategies to manage this?

- Do your two year olds have access to opportunities where they can replicate adult activities which they have observed? Being able to represent your ideas, particularly in visual and practical ways when you don't have lots of language to articulate those ideas is an important consideration.

- Walk around your setting as if you were a visitor or new family. What do you see that makes you know that you and your children are welcome here? Is information presented in ways that make it easy for you to understand and contribute to?

Useful resources

The resources used to create these 'places to talk' were easy to source, often inexpensive and enhanced existing provision.

Some of the items included:

- Bark, tree stumps, large tyres and interesting plants
- Collections of natural materials presented on an appropriate scale
- Canopies, various textures, drapes, cushions and bean bags
- A variety of lighting sources to add mood and atmosphere
- 'Real' resources offering tactile experiences
- Recycled perspex
- Pallets and bamboo guttering
- Real tools
- Pots, pans, whisks and sieves
- Sofas, benches and outside seating

Further references and useful websites

The Communication Friendly Spaces™ Approach Toolkit 2009, Elizabeth Jarman
www.elizabethjarmantraining.co.uk

Revised EYFS (2012) Statutory Framework and Development Matters
http://www.education.gov.uk/schools/teachingandlearning/curriculum/a0068102/early-years-foundation-stage-eyfs

A Know How Guide: The EYFS progress check at two
http://www.foundationyears.org.uk/early-years-foundation-stage-2012

Center on the Developing Child – Harvard University
http://developingchild.harvard.edu/topics/science_of_early_childhood/
Particularly: InBrief: The Science of Early Childhood Development

Young Children Learning Through Schemas (Katey Mairs and the Pen Green Team, London: Routledge, 2012)

Working with babies and children from birth to three (Cathy Nutbrown and Jools Page, Sage Publications 2008)

Getting it Right for Boys (Neil Farmer, Featherstone Education 2012)

Children's Outdoor Play & Learning Environments: Returning to Nature
http://www.whitehutchinson.com/children/articles/outdoor.shtml

Theory of Loose Parts
http://openlearn.open.ac.uk/mod/oucontent/view.php?id=406566§ion=4

About the author

Elizabeth Jarman is a leading Early Years professional specialising in creating really effective learning environments. She is the founder and managing director of the ELIZABETH JARMAN® Group. Her company is the sole provider of the Communication Friendly Spaces™ Approach which supports communication skills, emotional well-being and increased levels of engaged learning for children across all key stages. Elizabeth's work is widely recognised and respected. Her thinking is professionally challenging the way that environments for children are viewed.

Elizabeth has a background in teaching and worked as an Assistant Director for the Basic Skills Agency where she led national programmes on behalf of the Department for Education.

In Europe, Elizabeth has experience working as lead UK consultant with UNESCO advising on the development of Family Learning schemes. She is currently overseeing a project in Malta on home contexts environments. In The US, Elizabeth is leading an action research project working with Early Intervention Centers in Ohio.

Working with architects and educators, Elizabeth leads an international team of experts who deliver training and consultancy, develop resources and commission research on improving learning environments. She has a particular interest in engaging families in children's learning. Elizabeth writes for the education sector press and has published a number of books on Communication Friendly Spaces™.

Thanks to all of the schools, parents/carers and practitioners who informed and inspired this publication, especially:

Holmewood Nursery School and Children' Centre, Brixton, UK
Townsend Children's Centre, Bournemouth, UK
Woodpeckers Pre-School, Kent, UK
Red Roofs Private Day Nursery, Southampton, UK
Jacky Walker, Childminder, Weymouth, UK
Rosemary Albone, ELIZABETH JARMAN®, UK